# Gold Our Greatest Hits

By Lee, Claire, Lisa, H and Faye

First published in Great Britain in 2001
by Virgin Publishing Ltd
Thames Wharf Studios
Rainville Road
London W6 9HA

Copyright © Steps 2001
Interviews by Jordan Paramor

Colour Origination by Colourwise Ltd

A catalogue record for this book is available from the British Library.

ISBN 1 85227 922 2

# STEPS

## Gold Our Greatest Hits

By Lee, Claire, Lisa, H and Faye

# Contents

Wow, here we are again! Another year, another book, another album and another tour. We still can't believe how incredible it is being in Steps, and once again we want to say a massive thank you to all of you for making all of this possible.

We've had the most amazing time over the past few years, travelling the world, making videos and creating songs. We feel that one of the secrets of our success is the fact that we've enjoyed everything we've done so much, and we hope that by doing that we bring a bit of Steps sunshine into the lives of everyone who listens to our records, reads our books, watches our videos, or comes to see us in concert.

Just to make sure you really know how much you're all appreciated, we've decided to celebrate the life of Steps so far by bringing you a whole Greatest Hits extravaganza in the shape of Gold: the album, the tour and of course, the book! Read on to discover which of our tracks are our favourites and discover some of our best-kept tour and video secrets!

We want you to think of Gold as the end of the first chapter of the Steps story – and the beginning of a new exciting one! We've all still got so many ambitions and dreams we want to fulfil, and we know that with the support of you, our loyal fans, we can do just about anything.

# 5-6-7-8

RELEASED: 17 NOVEMBER 1997 / UK PEAK POSITION: 14 / UK CERTIFICATION: SILVER

**H**
Even though it's the only one of our singles that didn't go top ten, it still did brilliantly. It stayed in the charts for a ridiculous amount of weeks and sold masses more than anyone expected, especially as it was our first single and it didn't have a lot of airplay.

**Lisa**
5,6,7,8 wasn't what I expected at all. It had a country feel to it and I thought it was very catchy. I also thought it was either going to be a massive hit or a massive flop!

**Claire**
I first heard 5,6,7,8 at the audition and I didn't twig that it was going to be the single. When I realised I was a bit like, 'Oh, okay!'

**Lee**
Obviously all our early memories are about 5,6,7,8. That time was all about travelling around the country to nightclubs doing gigs. The first nightclub we ever played was in Swansea and we were so nervous standing there with all these people staring at us. We were there performing this pop line dancing song and people were looking at us as if to say, 'What on earth are they doing?'!

**Claire**
Whenever I hear the fiddle at the beginning of 5,6,7,8 it reminds me of the early days when we would stand with our backs to the audience, ready to perform. I'd be standing there thinking, 'Oh no, they're going to laugh at us'.

**Faye**
It was so weird going into nightclubs and performing a line-dancing track in a little skirt and high heels. People didn't really know how to take us. It was very bizarre. There were loads of trendy songs out at the time, and they would play them all before we went on stage so we'd have to psyche ourselves up and tell ourselves that people would be nice to us.

**Lee** We were so nervous. People can either take the mickey out of you or really like you, but at that early stage we weren't sure what was going to happen. It could have gone either way so we were a bit scared.

**Claire**
Thankfully nobody ever booed us off stage, which I found very strange! I thought we would have been booed off at least once. Thank god we weren't, though. I think I would have cried on the spot.

**Faye**
We were OK in the under-18s clubs because people would dance along, but when we did the over-18s clubs some people would just stare. Us girls did get cheered on by lots of blokes though!

**Lee**
We filmed the video on the beach in Marbella and we had to have this tape around where we were filming so that no one would disturb us. We also had loads of extras, which was quite cool and pop starry. I remember H and I got to ride these quad bikes on the beach, which was great. I had a lot more to do in that video than I probably have done in more recent ones because there were two raps. Well, if you can call them raps! I'd never done any rapping before and I enjoyed it but I'm not much of a rapper!

**H**
I loved those quad bikes, they were wicked. They used a shot of me spinning the wheels with all the sand going everywhere and it was so cool.

**Lisa** This was my first ever video so it was very exciting and I really enjoyed it. I think from then on I've always loved doing them.

**Faye**

Filming the video for 5,6,7,8 was one of the scariest things I've ever done because it was all so new. It was hard trying to be sexy dressed in a bikini because there were loads of people staring at us. It was our first taste of being pop stars and I definitely wasn't confident about it. It was scary because we didn't want to look silly. But we just tried to do our best and it was certainly hard work.

**Claire**

I wasn't that nervous making the video because I'd done a couple when I was in a band before. But we were all really excited about going abroad. We had a day off before the video shoot so we all went to sunbathe, but the director kept trying to make us go inside in case we got sunburnt. He kept coming and prodding us and telling us that we were going red. We pretty much ignored him!

**Faye**

We thought doing the video was so very glamourous, despite the fact that when us girls do the close-up shots we were actually standing in front of some toilet doors!

**Lisa**

We had a Spanish hairdresser for the shoot and I asked her to make my hair a bit wild, but she went a bit over the top. She used nearly a whole can of hairspray on it and it was massive. I felt ridiculous.

**H**

I remember being so excited filming the video because it was my first as well. And I remember pulling up to the airport to fly to Spain and we had our own driver standing there with a board that said 'Steps'. I felt so showbiz. I'm kind of used to it now but I still remember how good that felt.

**Claire**

We had a total nightmare with the hair and make-up people. I had one of those zig-zag-style clips in, and the hairdresser put it up really high and backcombed it. I'm not joking, I looked like a lion. I remember Lisa and I running to the portaloo and trying to tame our hair down. It looked a total mess in the video. My outfit was awful as well. I had an orange bikini, and I also had a red mesh top and red PVC trousers. Not a good look!

**H** We worked really hard on the video and we were extremely hot because it was so sunny and gorgeous. We kept having to fan ourselves in between takes.

# Last Thing On My Mind

RELEASED: 17 APRIL 1998 / UK PEAK POSITION: 6
UK CERTIFICATION: SILVER

**Claire**
When we first heard Last Thing On My Mind we thought it was a demo. We didn't realise it was the Bananarama version! We were all really worried about recording it but our manager told us to trust him and we did. Thankfully it turned out brilliantly. We were all in the studio at our producers' offices on chart day listening to the rundown.
I cried when we found out we were at number six. I cried when we found out where One For Sorrow had charted as well. How sad am I?

**Lee**
Getting to number six was a big push forward for us. 5,6,7,8 entered at 18 and its highest position was 14, so for the second single to enter at six was a big leap. I think that kind of made people sit up and take notice of us.

**Lisa**
We were so chuffed to be Top 10. And our record company were happy that we'd improved on 5,6,7,8 because it meant that we weren't just a one hit wonder. We were so relieved.

**Faye**
It was great to move on from the line-dancing and Last Thing On My Mind felt like the first proper pop song we did. I still like performing it on tour because everyone seems to love it.

**Lisa**
We couldn't believe our luck with this video. We'd only been together for a few months and there we were being flown out to Cuba for a week! We weren't expecting it at all. It was amazing and a bit like a holiday because we only filmed for two days. The rest of the time we sunbathed on the beautiful beaches. We had quite a few locals as extras so we used to go out with them in the evenings and we made quite a few new friends. Lee and I learnt our first bit of Spanish then as well. We were very proud.

**H**
The first time I ever tasted lobster was in Cuba, and it's one of my favourite foods now.

**Faye**
Look out for Lee's Cuban heels next time you watch the video. No one ever notices, but you've got to check them out. Then again I can't talk, I'm wearing those tiger boots.

**H**
It wasn't all glamour in Cuba. We stayed in this big hotel and there was this beauty queen competition going on there. Because there was nothing else to do in the city Claire and I ended up sitting and watching all these pouting girls parading down a catwalk.

H Last Thing On My Mind was kind of the tester single for us, really. Our first single had done well but this was the one that would say everything because it was the follow-up single. I don't think I was that nervous about releasing it, though, because I was enjoying myself so much. I was just going with the flow. I really like the song even now. It was a great summer tune and will be for many years. I still hear it played on the radio now and it's a great party song.

**Claire**
I liked Cuba but the plane ride out there was an absolute nightmare. We went with this really small airline which allowed smoking. We asked for non-smoking seats but it was so full we couldn't get them, and I also got separated from everyone. I closed my eyes during take off and when I opened them again everyone was smoking these really smelly cigarettes. It was disgusting. Then on the way back we flew via Madrid. We all went to go and collect our cases after the flight but mine never came through. I was absolutely gutted. I lost everything. I got it back about four months later, but in the meantime I'd been out and bought a whole new wardrobe and new Walkman and CDs and stuff. These days I never pack things like a Walkman in my case. I take it all in a separate bag so if I lose my suitcase I haven't lost everything. Sometimes I have so many extra bags the others say I look like a bag lady!

**Faye** I felt really glam doing the video. It was more set up than 5,6,7,8 and we felt much more confident doing it. Also, it was the same director that did 5,6,7,8 so we felt really comfortable with him. There was one bit where we had to drive along the street and pretend to laugh, and at first we couldn't do it because it's so hard to laugh on cue. But then it got to the point where we couldn't stop! We were crying with laughter and even after the scene had finished we were in fits. I enjoyed that video so much.

# One For Sorrow

RELEASED: 21 AUGUST 1998 / UK PEAK POSITION: 2
UK CERTIFICATION: GOLD

**Claire**
I liked the song from the beginning although it was never supposed to be a single. It was just going to be an album track. I remember when we recorded it. I was still doing vocals on it at about three or four o'clock in the morning because I was on a roll. Then a few days later Pete Waterman said he was going to play us the new single and he played One For Sorrow. We were all really shocked – but it's a great song.

**Lisa**
One For Sorrow put us on a new high – we were so pleased with how well it did because it really felt like ours. It was written for us, it wasn't a cover, and that made it really special. We felt like we'd found our sound and it spurred us on.
It brought us all together and made us feel like we all knew where we were going and what we wanted.

**Faye**
One For Sorrow always reminds me of summer. We went to Spain and performed it for GMTV and it was such a laugh – sun, fun and Steps.

**H**
Everyone does this dance when we're on tour because it's so easy. You look out into the crowd and absolutely everyone is doing it! It's the same as Tragedy. Everyone does that dance routine as well because they can do it even if they're sitting down!

**Faye**
There's a fantastic American mix of One For Sorrow that we perform a lot and I prefer that version, so make sure you check it out!

**Claire**
Faye, Lisa and H got dragged back from their holidays to film this video. It was all a real rush for them but because Lee and I went out to Italy before them we did most of our bits early and got to spend a lot of time in the sun!

**Faye**
I was in Greece and I got a phone call telling me that I had to be in Italy the next day, so my plane ticket got changed and my holiday was cut short. I was very upset but it was worth it in the end.

**Lee** I think One For Sorrow was a huge turning point for us. It entered the charts at number two and only just missed out on being number one to the Manic Street Preachers. We were doing a gig up in Liverpool on the Sunday it charted and we were listening to the radio to see where we'd gone in at. My parents were there and everything, and we even put off going on stage for five minutes so we could listen to our chart position. We were so made up to be number two that we were on a real high when we went on stage. We were a bit gutted about not getting to number one because there was only about a thousand copies between us and the song that beat us, but it still felt like an incredible achievement.

**H**

I had to rush back from Spain to go to Italy. That would never happen nowadays. I think we'd all put our foot down a bit! We stayed in this tiny little hotel in Italy and we didn't have towels, we had these teacloth-type things to dry ourselves. Very nice.

**Lee**

We filmed the video on Lake Garda in Italy. We used the grounds of this Countess's ancestral home and it was quite cool. It's one of the most popular videos, which I think is partly to do with the dance routine.

**H**

We were supposed to film the video by this beautiful lagoon that had palm trees and everything, and also in this really beautiful old Italian castle. But the day before we got there there was this tornado and the castle was damaged, the lagoon was a muddy pond, and all the palm trees collapsed. So we ended up in sunflower fields in front of some sewage works. It was great visually but I'm glad it wasn't smellavision because the sewage works stank.

**Claire**

The bugs out in Italy were disgusting. I'm so squeamish and when Faye and I had to walk through the long grass I was grabbing her hand and screaming because I was so scared.

**Lisa**

There were loads of insects around, and as I put my arm up to do the dance routine one stung me under my arm. It was so incredibly painful but I kept going and kept smiling until we'd finished the dance routine, then I ran to get some cream. H laughed at me as usual!

**Faye** Lisa got stung by a hornet! It was really hot and muggy and there were insects flying up our skirts. It was absolutely minging but we had to keep smiling and look like we were having the time of our lives. The out-takes from the video must have been hilarious because as soon as we finished the scene we'd be running around screaming like nutters!

# Tragedy

**Faye**
Tragedy has been the biggest and longest-running single we've had. It was big everywhere and it was our first British number one. Thank you!

**Claire**
It was in the charts for about eight or nine weeks before it got to number one. We weren't expecting it to be number one and we were completely chuffed. It was brilliant.

**Lisa**
Tragedy is a favourite of mine because personally I think we did a really good version. And obviously because we had so much success with it worldwide we will always be thankful. When Tragedy kicked in everywhere, that was when I stopped and thought, 'God, I'm really a pop star'! It was just amazing.

**H**
I remember the song from when I was a kid and I really liked it.

**Faye**
Tragedy is a bit of a thumb-print on Steps' music and a lot of people know us for that song. We recorded it for a charity album Bee Gees style! We were in the studio and the boys had to sing really, really high and we were mucking around taking the mickey out of them. But the end result was fab and a great success.

**Lisa** I think our audience grew and changed with Tragedy. We were doing a lot of university gigs at the time and everyone would join in and do the dance. So as well as having the kids loving it, we had older people getting down to it and enjoying the song. We even got Prince Charles doing the dance at Party In The Park, so the fantastic memories of Tragedy will always stay with me.

**Lee**
Tragedy took us to the next level. It was our first number one along with Heartbeat, and I think everyone in the world knows the dance routine. Thankfully people have stopped coming up to me and doing it all the time. I knew the song before we recorded it and I really liked the stage version of it, although it's very, very different. It's very slow and it's just a solo voice. The Bee Gees seemed to like our version, though. They even sent us a fax to say thank you and told us how great they thought it was. That was very cool.

**H**
I loved the fact that we got a fax from the Bee Gees. I was very excited. I went to see the stage show of Saturday Night Fever a while ago and Tragedy is in it. It's a ballad in the show and it's supposed to be a really sad moment when one of the cast members dies, but everyone in the audience was doing our Tragedy dance moves along to it. It was so funny.

**Claire**
We had our friends and family in the video because the budget was so small, but I think having them there made it more genuine. It was freezing that day and we had no dressing rooms or anything, but we had a really good time. My dad walked me down the aisle and my sister was my bridesmaid. It was so funny.

**Faye**
Filming the video was lovely, especially as my dad had tears in his eyes when we were walking up the aisle because I was in a wedding dress. He was getting all choked up and I had to say to him, 'Don't worry dad, I'm never going to get married'. But look at me now!

**Lisa** I really enjoyed making this video because I was surrounded by my family – a rare treat! I remember sitting in this beautiful Rolls-Royce with my Dad on our way to the church and we had to keep circling it because we were too early. We kept passing a couple of old ladies at a bus stop and it got a bit embarrassing after fifteen minutes or so. My Dad and I started ducking down in the car – we were sure that the ladies thought I'd been stood up!

**Claire**

I remember we went out and bought beer and wine for everyone to say thank you at the end of the shoot. I think all they got all day were some sandwiches so a lot of them nipped off to the local pub during takes!

**Lee**

Tragedy was actually one of the cheapest videos we've ever made but it looked fantastic. It was great to have our friends and family involved and I have some brilliant memories of the day when I look back on it. Especially how weird it was seeing all the girls in their wedding dresses!

**Faye**

I wore a fantastic headdress and it felt like I was looking out from a beaded curtain! The funny thing was I kept catching my false eyelashes on the beads – not very attractive! Interestingly enough, Edele and Keavy from B*Witched called me up to find out where it was from because their older sister was getting married and she wanted to get one. I don't know if she wore one in the end.

**Claire**

I remember having a trying on session in someone's flat and we were all trussed up in all different wedding dresses. Lisa went for something really traditional, Faye got something more modern, and mine was just terrible! I hated it, I thought I looked ridiculous. I kept trying to hide during the shoot!

**H**

I loved driving the scooter up and down the aisle in the video. I kept disappearing in between takes because I was driving it up and down the road! I've got my own scooter now. I drive it down to the video shop and to get a pizza, so I can often be seen out and about on my scooter with a pizza and a video balanced on the back.

**H** People still do the Tragedy dance moves to me all the time. But I kind of like it. All my friends still do it to take the mickey out of me.

# Heartbeat

RELEASED: 6 NOVEMBER 1998 / UK PEAK POSITION: 1 / UK CERTIFICATION: PLATINUM

**Faye** I always laugh when I watch the Heartbeat video because of H's 'brilliant' acting performance when he's being prodded by the extras. It's the same in the fight scene with the Snow Queen when everyone is trying to do karate. I wore a catsuit, which was very daring for me. Then again, it wasn't the last time.

**H** We filmed the video in West London and it was a two day shoot. It was pretty long and exhausting. We filmed a lot of it in front of a blue screen, which is where you act out the scenes in front of a colour and an image is substituted for the colour behind you. Very technical! You can't wear the same colour background as the screen. For instance if you wore blue gloves you wouldn't have any hands. So if I stuck a blue plaster on my mouth I wouldn't have a mouth. The rest of the band would love that!

**Lee**
Heartbeat holds the same memories for me as Tragedy because it was a double A-side. I remember it being played on the radio and I was really excited – we hadn't heard our songs being played that often because we'd been so busy.

**Lisa**
Heartbeat complemented Tragedy well because it was slower. It was a lovely song. It was our first ballad and I think people saw that there was more to us and we could do ballads as well as up-tempo songs.

**Faye**
This is my Steps Christmas song. It gives me a nice warm feeling when we sing it. Everyone loves singing along to it when we perform it in concert.

**Lee**
Heartbeat and Tragedy became number one for the new year which was an amazing way to start 1999.

**Faye**
I think Heartbeat was the first time we got a chance to really sing out on a single because all the others had been fast. It's really weird listening to it now and hearing how much our voices have changed.

**Lisa**
The video was a real laugh to film. It was all very tongue-in-cheek and we had a lot of fun with the extras. We seemed to be laughing all day. I had the task of doing a high kick on the wicked Snow Queen and it had to be really high because she was a six-foot-tall model!

**H**
The others always take the mickey out of my acting in that video. The director told me to look scared when the extras are beating me up, and they all laugh at my facial expressions. I remember that one of the extras was pregnant at the time, and I went to a panto recently and a few of them were in it, including her, so I went backstage to say hello. It was lovely to see them again.

**Lee**
This was our first effort at being super-heroes and it was a real comic book video. It was really cliched but a lot of fun.

**Faye**
We're really taking the mickey in that video, running around being silly. It wasn't like work at all.

**Claire**
We'd had such a busy summer and we were all exhausted by the time we came to film the video. I remember being up on the jet ski in front of the blue screen. I'm terrified of heights but I had to look like I was having a great time and was really cool with it. Arrrggghhhh! I had purple hair in this video. I've stopped dyeing my hair now. I've made so many dyeing mistakes and it's a nightmare to try and get rid of colour once you've got it, so I'm going to stick to blonde from now on. No more purple for me!

# Our Theatre Tour

## Lisa

This was our first tour and we were all very excited and nervous. We opened on the first night in Rhyl which was my home town, so I was twice as nervous because I knew that all my family and friends and dancing teachers and teachers from school would be there watching me. When I stepped out on stage I looked out in the audience and I knew everyone. I felt my stomach knot. The opening night actually turned out to be the best night for me, though. We did the show and then had a party backstage which was full of my family and friends and old dancing friends. It was like a big reunion for me. It was lovely.

## Claire

I played all of the theatres we played on our first tour when I was in my first band. But I used to have to stand in front of a black curtain back then. So the first time we got to go out as the main act and know that the show was ours was fantastic. I absolutely loved it.

## H

Being on stage is the reason a lot of us got into this business, so we were so happy being out on the road. People think that being in a band is all about performing, but it's actually probably only about 20% performing and 80% talking about it!

## Lee

I think we surprised a lot of people with the tour and it helped to elevate us higher in people's estimations.

## Faye

We were so surprised that we sold out all the theatres – it was such a big triumph because we had been criticised by a lot of people. But it proved to us that audiences out there did like us and that we had a lot of support.

## H

When the tour sold out it was such a brilliant feeling. The best.

## Lisa

This tour was even more special for me because it was where I first met my fiancé Johnny, as he danced for us. He's a fab dancer. We spent a lot of time together and got close, so this will always be my favourite tour because of those memories. I also met a girl called Lisa who was dancing for our support act Christian Fry, and she dances for us now. She's one of my best friends so it reminds me of her as well. I met a lot of good people then and we all enjoyed singing live and being on stage every night. Finally after two years we'd got what we wanted, which was a big successful tour.

**Faye**

We decided to do a Disney medley in the middle of the show and sing on our own so that everyone could see that we could sing live. I did Pocahontas and it was a real giggle. I've still got the dress and bag at home. I've even used the bag to go out a couple of times! I don't think I'll be wearing the dress out, though.

**H**

My favourite bit about this tour was the Disney medley. We all got to do our favourite Disney character and I was Simba from the Lion King. I used to come in balancing on the back of one of the dancers. I'm surprised I didn't fall off all the time!

**Lee**

I was Aladdin in the Disney medley, that was cool. I had a little sash around me and everything. H and I sang a song called Hero and we wore purple T-shirts with 'L' and 'H' on them. We kind of had to do that because at that time some people didn't know our names! It wasn't like it is now. The costumes were really simple and brightly coloured. Nothing like they are now with all our leather and studs!

**Faye**

We went out quite a lot on the tour. We went to some quite strange places around the country. I remember this one night we went bowling and Claire got told off for buying a drink because they thought she was underage.

**H**

We had some good nights out on that tour. I guess it was a time when we were getting to know each other so it was really special.

**Lee**

I don't remember us having too many wild parties. I'm more of a party dude now than I was then. I go out a lot more these days.

**Lee** The tickets sold out really quickly, which was quite scary as well as exciting. The sets were quite small with revolving doors, and there were three ladders at the back so we could use top and bottom sets to vary things a bit. We had five dancers, three boys and two girls to balance out the band, so we all had a dancer each.

41

# H I have to say, I did hate the tour bus. It was so bouncy and uncomfortable and I was much happier in hotels. I didn't sleep on the coach at all.

**Faye**
It was great getting to visit so many new places. Lisa and I managed to do quite a lot of partying. We made a pact that we would find a club in every town and try it out, and we did pretty well! We weren't that well known back then so we could walk down the street and not be recognised. And we could spend the night in a club without getting hassled so we could have a good boogie. We pretty much partied our way around the country.

**Lisa**
Faye and I did quite a lot of partying on this tour, as we did on every tour. I do think you should work hard and play hard, and I make sure I do! You've got to have a balance in life. I make sure I can always do a good job the next night, but I certainly enjoy myself.

**Claire**
We all travelled on the tour bus and as soon as we got on there every morning I would get into my bunk and go to sleep! Being on the tour bus was a good way of us lot getting to know each other. We would chat and watch videos and mess about, and it was a good laugh.

**Faye**
We all went on a tour bus back then because we didn't have our Previa cars and stuff. We weren't trying to get to venues as soon as possible and get some time off back then, we were just taking it slow and enjoying it. It was so nice to be out on the road doing our own thing. It was also good to have a proper schedule so we knew when we had to get up and if we could go out partying!

# Better Best Forgotten

RELEASED: 8 MARCH 1999 / UK PEAK POSITION: 2 / UK CERTIFICATION: GOLD

**Claire**
I liked Better Best Forgotten a lot. I loved the verses because they were quite low which meant they were nice to sing. The fans go mad when we perform this live on tour so we love doing it.

**Faye**
We can never remember the dance routine to this for some reason. We still have to have rehearsals for it now even though we've performed it tons of times.

**Lee**
I have to admit that this song probably is Better Best Forgotten for me as it's my least favourite of all our songs. I've got a bit of thing about it. But it's one of the fans favourites so I still enjoy performing it, but I think it makes us sound like chipmunks!

**Faye**
I still want to know what the bit at the beginning of the song is. You know, that 'woaoaoaoao' bit, because it's not me singing! Is it a chipmunk? Is it a Smurf? I just don't know. Answers on a postcard, please.

**Lisa**
This is a funny one because it's not one of my favourites but it is still hugely popular with the fans. I go on our official website a lot and they all seem to still love it which means I really enjoy it when we're performing it.

**Claire**
I must admit, I didn't really like this video that much. I don't think very much happens.

**H**
This was one of our near misses. If we'd released it at any other time it would have been number one.

**Faye**
It was a very dramatic song. It was the last song we released from the first album, Step One, and it brought it to a close. It was one of our biggest selling singles from the first album and it's still a favourite.

**H**
The video was filmed in the same studio as Heartbeat. Nobody really knew what they were doing on the shoot. We kind of improvised and made it up as we went along.

**H**
I was wearing what looked like a blue bin liner for a costume, which is always nice. I had to do all my shots first because the outfit was so hot I was dripping in sweat, so they wanted to get me out of the way!

Best
ten

**Faye** The video for Better Best Forgotten holds memories of me having glass stuck in my bottom. When we were filming we had a mock-up of a glass tiled wall behind us, and it fell on me halfway through a verse. It smashed and I got splinters in my bum and a sore head.The crew had to use this airbrush thing and then pick the splinters out with tweezers! I was supposed to be being glamorous in my genie outfit with my hair done up all nicely, but instead I was lying there with my backside out for all to see! Well, almost.

Lee I remember Faye lying there and having the glass picked out of her bum. Something I'm sure every guy would love to do! She was so cool about it, though. She didn't panic at all. She's dead hard, our Faye! I don't think we would all have been that cool if it had happened to us.

**Lisa**
Blimey, I remember when the set fell down on Faye! She was really brave about it.

**Claire**
I didn't even know Faye had been injured. I'd done my bit so I'd gone and locked myself in a room to get away from everything and have a rest. When I came out later someone asked me how Faye was and I didn't have a clue what they were talking about. When someone told me they were picking splinters of glass out of Faye I panicked, but luckily she was fine.

# Love's Got A Hold On My Heart

RELEASED: 12 JULY 1999 / UK PEAK POSITION: 2
UK CERTIFICATION: SILVER

**Faye**
This song reminds me of when we went on a TV show that Eartha Kitt was also on. She was bonkers. She was totally off her rocker but I had to get her autograph because she's a real legend. We were standing around backstage and she walked past us and stood in this doorway and said: 'Well, when you get to my age, darling'. Then she growled, stuck her leg in the air, squealed, and ran off. We just stood there stunned. She was very eccentric, just fantastic.

**Lee**
This song reminds me of summer sunshine. We wore bright yellow in the video and to be honest, that's the only thing I don't like about it. I think we looked like five canaries! I blame Faye because it was her idea as she loves yellow and gold. We all went with it because we hadn't done it before but I thought I looked a bit ridiculous, like Big Bird.

Heart

**Faye**
One word described the video – yellow. It was filmed in Cannes and it was like a big yellow Enid Blyton mystery with us running around trying to find our stolen film reels. We felt so incredibly glamorous because we had all these Winnebagos – massive plush caravan things – outside, so people kept looking to see who we were. It was just after the film festival so there were still quite a lot of film stars around and we were very excited. We felt very important!

**Claire**
The yellow outfits are the ones we're always remembered for, probably because they were so bright. Whenever anyone takes the mickey out of us or impersonates us they always wear yellow outfits.

**H**
Cannes is one of my favourite places. I'd been on holiday there before so I knew a lot of places to go.

**Faye**
There were a lot of these Joan Collins-type ladies lying on the beach near where we were filming and they looked just the part. They had big hair and shades and were incredibly glamorous. We found them very amusing and we couldn't help staring!

**Lisa** The video took us two days to film in all, and we had such a good time because it was such a lovely place. I liked Cannes a lot and we got to have half a day off so we all went and sunbathed on the beach. Us girls are proper sun worshippers so we were well happy.

## Lisa

I immediately think of yellow when I think of this video. It was very bright and summery and was great for the time, but I don't think you'll get us wearing yellow again now. I remember doing the dance routine on the pier and it was a beautiful day but very windy and H and I were being a bit vain and panicking about our hair. I'd dyed my hair red and I wanted it to stay that way so in between takes H and I were hiding underneath a huge parasol that we had pulled down right over our heads. People could only see our bodies and we looked ridiculous.

## H

Lisa and I hid for ages. Our eyes kept stinging whenever we went out into the wind so we stayed under there for as long as possible. We also used to go for a wander along the fountains in between takes as well, because it was so beautiful – we didn't want to waste too much time hiding! Lisa and I went for a walk during one break and saw this pet shop that had all these gorgeous puppies in the window. I remember that we went back and told Claire and she was so upset because she didn't have time to go and see them. I'd love a dog, but I can't have one because of all the travelling we do. I've got two cats, though. I got them from a rescue centre called the Mayhew in West London. They're brothers. One's black and he's called Dylan after Dylan Thomas, and the other one is white and he's called Hugo because he's the boss! I was going to call them Ant and Dec but I changed my mind at the last minute.

## Claire

I wore a dress in this video which was very unusual for me. I don't know what was going on there! I remember being so upset on the day we shot the video. I'd just had hair extensions put in and this French hairdresser put heated rollers in and frazzled the ends. I'd only had them in a few days because I had them put in specially for the video, and they cost a fortune. Someone tried to save them for me when I got back but they were totally ruined.

## Claire

Ricky Martin kept us off number one with Livin' La Vida Loca. He pulled this massive stunt in a record store in Oxford Circus and stayed at number one. It should have been us! We were in Canada on the Britney tour so we couldn't even do any promotion. It was a bit frustrating.

**Lee** Filming the video was great. We went to this hotel in Cannes which is one of the biggest hotels in the world. It was amazing. Apart from Heartbeat it was one of our first videos to have a story running through it. It was about us trying get the Steps movie back from these people who had stolen the film reels.

# Our First Arena Tour

**Claire** I call this the pyramid tour. It was a great show and I always remember standing at the back and waiting to run through the audience. There was such a build up. Then we would run up to the stage and everyone would go mad. It was such a nice feeling.

**H**
We started the whole show with a carnival and we used to come through the audience dressed up in these mad outfits carrying streamers and stuff. At first no one realised that it was us until we actually got on stage, but obviously some of the fans would come and see the show more than once so they soon knew what was going on. So as the shows went on they spotted who we all were and we got grabbed more and more. But it was all good fun!

**Faye**
It was a very demanding show because we had to run up and down the pyramid all the time. So not only were we doing all our dancing but we had to dance uphill and downhill as well! We all went to the gym beforehand to get ourselves fit for it.

**Lee**
We all thought the pyramid was amazing. It opened out on all different levels and things came out of it and everything. It was different because no one had used a set up like that before.

**Claire**
It was amazing to be doing our first arena tour. We were so unsure how it was going to sell, and we were worried because we would have been so embarrassed if it hadn't sold. It actually sold out incredibly quickly and we were all so chuffed.

**Faye**
We all felt like our hard work had paid off and we were getting to do the thing we really, really loved. What a buzz!

**Lisa** This was fantastic because it was an arena tour, and it seemed like only five minutes before that we were doing a theatre tour. We couldn't believe it had sold out and we felt really popular! I think we felt very loved and lucky as well.
We were so pleased that all these people wanted to come and see us, and it was nice to have the opportunity to perform and make people smile.

**H**
A lot of this tour was a bit a blur for me because I think I partied on most of it! We were all celebrating because the tour exceeded everyone's expectations and was the most incredible experience ever.

**Claire**
I also went out quite a lot on this tour. I remember sitting up in the bar with one of our dancers, Stuart, until five in the morning. It was getting light outside and we thought we had better get some sleep. I was pretty rock'n'roll on that tour!

**Lisa**
I celebrated my 23rd birthday on this tour. My birthday is on bonfire night and we happened to be at Wembley. Our agents Concorde and promoters AAA threw a party for me and there were fireworks and everything. It was amazing! And the rest of the band got the audience to sing Happy Birthday to me. It was very moving.

**H**
You can't beat the feeling of when you first come out on stage. Everyone starts screaming and it's electric. There's nothing else like it. It puts shivers up my spine and it makes me think, 'Yep, that's why I'm doing this'.

**H**
This was a step up for us. We thought we were going to do ten dates and we ended up doing about 35. It was the biggest ever arena tour in this country and was the start of selling over a million tickets. It was ridiculous!

**Faye**
Lisa and I did a lot of partying once again on this tour. We had quite a lot of dancers as well so we were going out clubbing with them a lot.

**Claire**
I remember the first time we played Wembley. I used to work there so it was very strange for me. I was fine the whole way through and then we got to Tragedy and everybody went crazy and I lost it. I was crying my eyes out. We all had our bits to say at the end and I was supposed to start it off by thanking everyone for coming, but I couldn't because I was crying so much! In the end someone else had to do it for me.

**Lee**

We did a live Sky show on that tour. We had a space buggy that was a converted golf cart. I drove it most of the time because they didn't trust anyone else to do it, but Lisa was determined to have a go of it so she got to drive it off every night. It was typical that the night we were being filmed she went to drive it off and it wouldn't go – live on Sky in front of millions of viewers! The next song was my solo song so they all left me and I just about managed to get it in gear and get it off the stage. Everyone was backstage panicking but luckily I covered it pretty well and I don't think anyone noticed.

**Lisa**

Someone had this idea to have a golf buggy and turn it into a space buggy. So we painted it silver and we had a bit in the show where we pretended we were in space and we performed Deeper Shade of Blue on it. H really wanted to drive it but he can't even drive a car so we told him he couldn't! We thought it was way too dangerous. In the end myself and Lee drove it. It was quite difficult because it wasn't like a normal car, and it was hard to drive it and sing at the same time. But I got better as time went on. That was a real highlight for me. I remember in rehearsals our choreographer Paul jumped into the buggy to demonstrate how it worked, but instead of going forward he whacked it into reverse and I was standing behind him so he knocked me over. I was nearly knocked out by the space buggy!

**Lee**

This was the first time I performed a solo song that I'd written. It was called Gonna Have A Party and it's actually on The Tweenies album now. They heard it and loved it and asked me if they could record it. It was such a good feeling performing it and it's what really stands out for me on that tour. We usually do everything as a group and I'd never got a chance to show what I could do on my own before so I felt like I'd proved a point. Especially as I'd written the track myself.

**H**

I did a version of George Michael's Careless Whisper on this tour. I started off doing it as a ballad like he does, and then it got really up-tempo. It had a fantastic dance routine and everyone used to go mad and sing along because it's such a classic.

# After The Love Has Gone

RELEASED: 11 OCTOBER 1999 / UK PEAK POSITION: 5
UK CERTIFICATION: SILVER

**H**
I really liked this song. It was very Abba and Claire did a brilliant vocal on it.

**Faye**
I thought After The Love Has Gone was a new version of One For Sorrow. A second part.

**Claire**
We flew down to Florida after the Britney tour to film the video. The album had only just been finished so we didn't know the song that well, so we kept messing up the words. The director was getting really annoyed and frustrated with us.

**Lisa**
I loved filming this because there was an oriental theme throughout the song and the video, and because my granddad's Chinese it was his favourite. Because I love him very much I thought it was lovely to do something Chinese and I think it made him really happy. I went to town on the outfit. I had a gorgeous green pyjama set with a dragon down it and it's still one of my favourite outfits that I've ever worn.

**Claire**
We learnt the dance routine the day before we made the video, and they wanted us to do all this high-kicking action stuff. I was praying they weren't going to make me do any of it because I would have made such a fool of myself. It's just not me at all. And I was wearing a dress – so it wouldn't have been a good move. In the end all I had to do was spin around this stick and trip this bloke up. Nothing too energetic.

**H** It was so cool filming the video on a real film set and it turned out really well. We all designed our own costumes and we got to do karate chops and stuff. I got to smack the bad guy in the face with a big wet kipper which was a good comedy moment.

**Lee** I did enjoy doing this one because it gave me a chance to do my martial arts. Also, H got to do some of the choreography which was cool.

**Faye**
I really enjoyed doing the martial arts training with the professionals and because I've been a dancer I'm fairly flexible so I didn't find it too hard. It was so amazing how highly skilled you have to be. Every time we touched any of the bad guys in the video they just flipped and ended up on the floor!

**Claire**
Lee loved this video because he got to do all his martial arts. We were all very impressed. It was brilliant.

**Lee**
We had about seven or eight stunt guys working with us so I got friendly with them and learnt a lot, especially during all the fight scenes. I was in my element being at Universal Studios because I'm such a film buff. I'd love to do acting some day. I know I'd love to combine martial arts with acting.

**Lisa**
It was great doing the video in America because it showed me how far we'd come. It was really exciting looking around Universal Studios and feeling like we were a part of it.

**Faye**
I loved being at Universal Studios because during lunchtime we ran off to go on the rides. My friend came out to stay with me so while we were shooting this video we sneaked off and we went on all the newest rides.

**Claire** We stayed at this hotel called The Peabody Hotel. And believe it or not, every day at ten o'clock they would roll out a red carpet and lead this family of ducks along the carpet and down to this fountain in the lobby. People used to gather round every single day just to watch the ducks walk along this carpet. It was very strange.

# Say You'll Be Mine

RELEASED: 13 DECEMBER 1999 / UK PEAK POSITION: 4
UK CERTIFICATION: GOLD

**Faye**
This was my favourite song for a long time because we all got to sing on it equally which was really, really nice. It was a big accomplishment for us.

**Faye**
I think this was one of the best video ideas in terms of the acting parts, but I wasn't keen on dancing in the gold outfits in between. I was allergic to my gold outfit as well because the material had a metal content in it and I've got a serious nickel allergy. It was a nightmare to wear.

**Lisa**
I wasn't very keen on this outfit. It was a gold two-piece with fringing identical to my Nana's lamp shade!

**Claire**
My top was held together with this clear elasticated stuff and it kept snapping every time I did the dance routine because it was a bit energetic!

**H**
This wasn't one of my favourite videos because of the fact that we all looked like gold lamp shades. Unfortunately we were so busy and tired we agreed to the outfits without thinking properly! I never regret anything, but if we could go back and do it all again that's the one thing I'd change.

**Faye**
I think I would have preferred the whole video to have been the film take-offs only because everyone did such a good job. Then again there's always that new dance routine to learn!

**H** I loved it when Claire and I did the Romeo and Juliet scene with the fish tank. There were so many funny out-takes from that shoot. The funniest stuff was the last scene of the day where Faye and I are doing Austin Powers. We'd had some champagne at that point because it was about two in the morning, and we were all giggly, especially as we weren't really sure what we were supposed to be doing.

**Lee**
This was the first song where we all got to sing a lead which was really important to all of us. I don't think any of us really liked the costumes in the video when we're dancing. My trousers were sprayed gold and they looked pretty terrible. We enjoyed acting out the roles, though. I was Batman, Ben Stiller from There's Something About Mary and Ben Affleck from Armageddon.

**Claire**
I loved the costumes I got to wear for the acting bits, although the red lycra dress I wore for the There's Something About Mary sketch felt a bit weird as it wasn't me at all. I loved playing Juliet in Rome and Juliet, but I must admit it was hard to keep a straight face when we were filming. I had to gaze lovingly at H through a fish tank and I kept laughing every time I looked at him. I had to keep stopping because I was giggling so much.

**Lisa**
It was a good laugh playing all the different characters. H and I had quite a few scenes together so there was a lot of laughing. We recreated the famous Titanic scene at the front of the boat – the set builders did a great job. There was one bit where H held out my arms and I was shouting 'I'm flying H, I'm flying'! It was just like the film. It was so cool.

**Faye**
It was just brilliant when H and I came to shoot our Austin Powers scene as well. We didn't really know a lot about the film as we hadn't had time to see it, so we improvised. And you know H! We were a bit overtired and he had me in stitches!

**Faye**
My other character in the video was Catwoman and I remember standing on the roof of the studio wearing a Catwoman outfit, high heels and a plastic hood with ears on thinking 'what on earth am I doing?' It tickles me every time I think about it.

**Lisa**
Everyone knows that H and I are a bit naughty when we're together. We get the giggles a lot, and we got them really badly that particular day. The director went mad because we'd been giggling for ages, and in the end he told us that we were wasting time and money. Unfortunately that made us giggle even more. There's a bit in the out-takes at the end where we're just laughing and laughing and I'm really glad they left it in. I have really good memories when I think back to that day.

# Better The Devil You Know

RELEASED: 13 DECEMBER 1999 / UK PEAK POSITION: 4 / UK CERTIFICATION: GOLD

**Lisa**
This was the first and only live video we've ever done. We didn't have much time because we were on our arena tour so we shot the video live on stage at Wembley!

**Faye**
We decided to do this song because we wanted to have a party record for Christmas.

**Lisa**
I'm always a bit wary of doing covers and think that unless you can better a song there's no point in doing them. It was Pete Waterman's idea to record Better The Devil You Know. He produced the original with Kylie and he knew what he was doing because it was a top five hit for us.

**Faye**
After we'd released Better The Devil we did a big outside show and Kylie came on and introduced us and it was really strange. I wonder what she thinks of our version?

**Claire**
This song is one of my favourites to perform. I always liked the song and I think we did a really good version of it. I liked it when Kylie did it, but obviously I prefer our version. I'm a bit biased, though!

**Lisa**
We all went to see Kylie in concert recently and she performed Better The Devil You Know, except she did a slowed down cabaret version. The ironic thing was that all the people in the audience were doing our dance moves to it!

**Lee**
I liked the Kylie version of Better The Devil You Know, but I really liked our version of it as well because we gave it a 90s twist. The thing most people remember about the dance routine is the shaking hands move.

**H**
We had mad outfits for this song, they're some of the most memorable we've ever had. I remember Faye hating the devils horns because they always used to fall off her head. But we all had to wear them so she had to participate as well. And poor Lisa's coat was so long she looked like Dopey from the Seven Dwarves! It totally drowned her.

**Lee**
I think it was a really good move doing a live video because people who hadn't seen us in concert got to see what we were capable of.

**Faye** This was the time of the flashing horns and every time you go to a Steps concert now you get tons and tons of people wearing flashing horns! They're fantastic if you're in the audience, but I had to be really persuaded to wear them, because let's just say they weren't my favourite thing. I literally had to be forced to wear them when we performed on the lottery – I wasn't a happy bunny!

# Deeper Shade Of Blue

RELEASED: 3 APRIL 2000 / UK PEAK POSITION: 4

**Faye** I think this is probably my all-time favourite video and song. It's so completely different to all our other videos. We really got into character and rather than us running around smiling, it was really nice to put on a special costume and do something new. I love the bit where H's arm falls off!

**Lee**
This was a twist to the Steps story. It was a new phase because we had a whole new image which was much harder. There was a different vibe and the track did really well in the club charts. The video took two days to film and it was all about Steps' alter-egos. It made people see us in a totally different light and I think that's the key to our career. We've always changed and evolved and we can be a lot of different people.

**Lisa**
This is one of my favourite songs because it's dancey and I love dance music. It was different for Steps. It was a real step up because it was a lot more grown up. I don't think people expected it from us at all so we surprised a lot of people. We really pushed the barriers in the video and we went further than we ever thought we would. It goes down a storm when we perform it. The crowd are electric whenever it starts playing.

**H**
I remember the scene so well where I'm lying in the blue sand with my arm falling off. It was so, so strange!

**Faye**
As much as I loved this video I was a bit gutted when I saw the final cut because there was supposed to be computer graphics on the whole thing and I was supposed to have that big blue swirly hair throughout. But I ended up with this short blue wig! I'm sure people who didn't know my hair was supposed to be long thought it looked fine, but I don't think I'm a short spiky person so it felt really strange watching it.

**H**
This is without a doubt one of my favourite songs and videos. It was quite a hard video for me because I was doing lead vocals, so I had to be there really early in the morning on the first day. Then I finished at about three the next morning and I had to be back on set at seven. I was so, so tired. Doing videos is really fun but they take ages. I slept for about three days afterwards.

**Faye**
The shoot took two days because the make-up and outfits were so extravagant. The rubber outfits were pretty horrible to wear. We had to put on talcum powder underneath them and we were sweating loads while we were filming. You know when you make papier-mâché and it goes like sticky glue? That's what we were covered in when we took off our costumes. Grim.

**Claire** I had a giant blue ponytail coming out of my head and our choreographer Paul said to me: 'I've just figured out who you look like. My Little Pony!' Of course, the boys found it absolutely hilarious. I had this lump of wood attached to the ponytail to make it stick out which wasn't terribly comfortable.

**Claire**
When they told me I was going to be wearing a catsuit I was like, 'No way!' It was all slashed up the side and showed off my thighs. It was very saucy. I was literally sewn into that costume. You know the plastic tags you get on clothes in shops? The stylist had a gun like that and she clicked me into the catsuit with those little tags. It was so tight, and the corset top was a proper old-fashioned corset. So once I was in it, that was it, and I was in it for about eight hours non-stop. I couldn't even go to the loo! We didn't even take our costumes off when we had dinner because we would never have got them back on again.

**Claire**
I wore these huge perspex shoes and dancing in them was impossible as I'm so used to dancing in trainers. It was probably the most uncomfortable video we'd ever made, but it did look amazing.

**Faye**
My video setting was a little stage surrounded by fluorescent lights to look like a cage. Paul the choreographer was getting me to do short, sharp movements and it was like doing 80s-style robotics. It was kind of cool. It was a bit more like a film than a video and I was really impressed with the end result.

**Lee** I like the fact that I got to show my strength in the video. I think a lot of people were surprised by my body because I hadn't really got it out before. They showed the video on a TV programme that Boy George was on and he said: 'Where has that boy been hiding his body?' That was cool.

**Lisa** The video definitely was uncomfortable to make. Firstly, because I was in a tiny little outfit and high heels, and secondly because I had to be painted completely blue for it. H actually painted my right arm because he's trained in art and wanted to help out. It took hours and hours to paint and then it took ages to get off again. I had five consecutive showers – I thought I was going to be blue forever!

**H** I remember going into the shower after Lisa. That's AFTER Lisa, not with her! She'd covered the whole place with blue dye and it looked mad. I really enjoyed helping to paint Lisa. There was so much going on so I thought I'd help out. I did art when I was younger and I miss it and am planning to get back into painting. We're always really creative with Steps. We all help to design the costumes for our videos, and when it comes to the tours we'll all have a brainstorming session about what we want and then I'll draw the sets. Very often the sets are made up from those drawings and it's amazing to see the whole process through to the end result.

**Lisa**

I don't think anyone can help but sing along to Deeper Shade Of Blue. In fact, not even I can! Johnny and I walked into a bar in Leicester Square and there was this song playing and I thought, 'Oooh, I like this one' and started singing along. It wasn't until I got to the chorus that I realised it was Deeper Shade Of Blue. Everyone was looking at me and I must have looked so sad singing along to one of our songs! Johnny was really laughing at me. I usually hide if our songs come on when I'm out because people always try and get me to show them the dance routines. I get really embarrassed!

# Our Second Arena Tour

**Claire**
This was a brilliant tour, I loved it. I thought it was such a good show. We're not particularly known for being cool but this was wicked. It was a bit darker and the costumes were a bit cooler.

**Lee**
We had what we called our 'Gotham City' set for this tour, with loads of metal bars and little streets. There were slides and stairways and steps and all sorts of stuff. We used to come down from the ceiling on a huge sphere at the beginning, and I used to stand on top of it, which was pretty dangerous.

**Claire**
I loved the opening when we came down from the ceiling to the dance mix of Deeper Shade Of Blue. There were pyros going off all over the place and it was just fantastic. I loved it, it was a fantastic feeling. But I must admit that I cried the first time we did it in rehearsals. I was like, 'I can't do it'. Then they told me that when we got into the arena it would be even higher and I totally panicked. I got through it, though. One night my seatbelt-thing wasn't attached properly. The fact that I was attached to the sphere was the only thing that made me do it, but it came undone halfway down and I was trying to smile while mouthing to the others, 'I'm not attached!'. I'll never forget that.

**H** This was the tour when I got to fulfil my dream and fly. I planned months and months ahead for this tour, and I'd been writing down all these ideas of what I wanted to do. I had this idea of coming down on a huge letter H but I never thought we'd be able to do it, but we did. So I used to come down on that and then fly and somersault over the audience. That was absolutely the highlight for me. I'd wanted to do it ever since I was really young.

**Faye**
I remember Claire had to be really persuaded to do the part where we came down from the ceiling as she's so terrified of heights. But she was brilliant about it, really cool.

**H**
The feeling of coming down from the ceiling was incredible. No one used to realise it was us until we got about halfway down and then everyone would start screaming.

**H**
We did a song called Things Can Only Get Better on this tour which was originally done by a band called D:Ream. A guy called Peter Cunnah wrote and sang the song and he surprised Lee and I by coming on stage in Manchester and singing it with us. I'm actually songwriting with him now which is brilliant.

**Lee**
This tour was part of the reason that we got a BRIT award and got into the Guinness Book Of Records. We sold over a million tickets and it's one of those phenomenal successes you read about. It's incredible that I was a part of it.

**Faye** My favourite bit about being in Steps is touring, so it was amazing getting to do such a massive tour. I love the fact that when you're on tour you know what time you're getting up, you get to sing live every night, and all your friends and family come to see you. Perfect. I love getting feedback from the fans as well. It's incredible to look out and see everyone singing back to you and doing all the dance routines.

**Lisa** Being on tour is the only time in our lives that we have a routine. Usually we never know what's going on from one day to the next! But on tour we get up and go to the gym, then we have lunch, then in the afternoon we do promotional work, then at five o'clock we do a sound check, at six o'clock we start doing our make-up and a vocal warm-up, then we're on stage at quarter to nine. It's the same every day, day in, day out, and it's the only time we have that stability and a normal daily routine, which I actually like.

**Lisa**
I wrote a song for the third tour called Never Get Over You with a well-known songwriter/producer called Ray Hedges. We all did solos on the tours and I was so excited when I got to perform mine. The beginning of the track started with wedding bells so I designed this wedding dress that had velcro down the front and back. Two of the dancers used to pull it off during the number and I had these spangly little hot pants, a chiffon top and glitter boots underneath. I was really proud of myself because I'd written the song, and I also thought about how I wanted to perform it and the costumes and everything. Everyone liked the song so much it ended up on the Buzz album which was a bonus and felt really good.

**Lee**
I got to do a solo song on this tour as well. It was a track called Come On Get Together that I'd written with a guy called Ray Hedges. I popped up from the middle of the stage and all these firework effects would go off. It was a really energetic song and I used to run around the stage belting it out.

**H**
It was my birthday during this tour and I had a fancy dress party in the bar backstage at Wembley. All my friends and family came down. Everyone had to come as an 80s pop star and I came as Adam Ant. In fact, most of my friends did as well! It was all by coincidence which was really weird. I remember when I did the splits on the dancefloor when I was messing about, and my trousers ripped from the waist at the back to the waist at the front. It was so embarrassing but I was just laughing and laughing.

**Lee**
Loads of people came to see us on that tour, like Dane Bowers, French and Saunders, Emma Noble and James Major, Denise Van Outen, Phil Jupitus and his kids, a couple of the Spice Girls, some of B*Witched and a couple of All Saints.

# Summer Of Love

RELEASED: 3 JULY 2000 / UK PEAK POSITION: 5

**Lee** This is a cool summer dance anthem. It's got the same feeling as Will Smith's Summertime. It's like it's saying 'Yay, summer's here, we can let our hair down and party!' It's got a nice little dance routine to it and a bit of a Latino theme. I think it will be played every summer for years.

**Claire**
I liked this song and funnily enough it always reminds me of summer! It makes me feel really cheery. I look forward to performing it because it's like the audience lifts when we do it on tour.

**H**
This is one of my favourite songs. It's a real feel-good party number and obviously very summery. It makes people feel really happy.

**Faye**
I thought this was a great Latino song and it always goes down really well in clubs.

**Lee**
We played 'Good Steps/Bad Steps' in the video. I was in leather with tattoos down my arms and spiky hair for bad Steps, and I was all smiley in a blue bandana and some nice bright clothes for the good Steps. It was cool to compare the two.

**Lisa**
We were inspired by the Gap adverts for this video. We had a white set and brightly coloured clothes which I think really worked. It was fun playing two different characters. For the darker side of Steps I had dark make-up and I wore a purple chiffon top and black three quarter length trousers and black boots. It was a bit of a raunchy look.

**Faye** I'd had my second lot of dreads put in when we did this video. I get bored with my hair so easily and I decided to do something with it again. This time they were the multicoloured ones and I didn't like them as much as the first ones I had done which were plain white. They took about eight hours to do in all and I was so bored by the end of the day! I actually did them for the second arena tour so that I wouldn't have to do too much to my hair during the tour. How lazy!

**H**

We went into the studio the night before the shoot and set up some shots for the camera. It was called a motion control camera and we had to fit two of ourselves into the shots. It was done by running a camera along a track and it was recorded every centimetre. Then they split the screen and put 'Good Steps' on one side and 'Bad Steps' on the other so they were both in the same shot. It's the same camera Britney uses in her Lucky video.

**Claire**

I loved the Bad Steps look, I think everyone looked great. We did a lot of the video in one take as we had a huge camera rigged up that would swing around and film us for ages at a time. That was something different for us.

**Faye**

It was like a dance-off in this video and we had a real laugh making it.

**Claire**

I made another hair mistake in this video. I decided to go for pink ends on my hair and it didn't really work. It was just spray for this video, but then I decided to go and have it done properly afterwards but it went all washed out and looked terrible. Yet another reason I've stopped dyeing it!

# When I Said Goodbye

RELEASED: 3 JULY 2000 / UK PEAK POSITION: 5

**H** This was a duet between Claire and I which was lovely. It's very different to what we usually do and was filmed in black and white which I thought fitted brilliantly with the romance of the song.

**Faye** Nobody was wearing any clothes in this video! We wanted to make it a really sophisticated ballad and Kenny Ho, our stylist at the time, persuaded us to wear these really saucy outfits which did look pretty sophisticated. We got a lot of wolf whistles when we were walking through the street to locations and stuff. I don't think you could really miss us! I had some straight hair extensions in this video. They were really easy to put in. They were just glued in like a wig. I loved them! I've got to be really careful what I do with my hair now though, because I colour it all the time and it's going to fall out one day I'm sure. I'm having to try and be really good.

**Claire**
I think it's a lovely song and I think a lot of people were shocked by it because it didn't seem to be very us. But I think it's beautiful. I liked this video because it was in black and white and it looked really romantic when we watched it back. Watching it reminds me of being there and how beautiful it was.

**Lisa**
I thought the song was lovely. We hadn't done a ballad for a while and people seem to respond really well to it when we do it live.

**Lee**
I see When I Said Goodbye as a step on from Heartbeat, really. Heartbeat was the only ballad we'd released before and this kind of took over from it. It was about lost love, and kissing and making up.

**Claire** I absolutely fell in love with Rome. It was just beautiful. There were so many amazing things there. I was first up to do my bit and it was really early in the morning and raining really hard. I was not pleased! I spent quite a lot of time hiding in the van.

**Faye**
I thought this was such a lovely song and it was great getting to sit down for a whole video. I remember all of us thinking how easy Westlife have got it because they get to sit down all the time! It was very strange not having to do a dance routine. I kept feeling like I should get up and dance.

**H**
Rome was one of the best places I've ever visited. One of my favourite films is The Talented Mr Ripley, some of which was filmed in the same places we filmed this video. I remember watching The Talented Mr Ripley afterwards and getting really excited spotting all the places we'd been to. I haven't been back to Rome since that video but I'd love to.

**Lee**
We stayed in Rome for a couple of days afterwards and got to see The Colosseum and all the amazing statues. It's an incredible place.

**Lee**
I remember Claire sitting on some steps with an umbrella because it started raining, and she was shivering in her little top.

**Claire**
I was wearing the skimpiest top in this video. It was basically just a length of suede sewn at one end and put through my belt loop. It was stuck on with so much toupee tape you wouldn't believe it.

**Lisa**
I remember hugging Claire to keep warm because we were both freezing!

# Stomp

RELEASED: 16 OCTOBER 2000 / UK PEAK POSITION: 1

**Faye** The video was a two-day shoot and we had loads of extras. We had a really hectic couple of days because we did the photo shoot for the single and interviews and everything at the same time.

**Faye**
I really, really liked this song. When we recorded it everyone was a bit dubious because it was a bit of a different style, but it turned out really well.

**Claire**
I love this song. I think it's wicked and it gets everyone up dancing. It's got a real party sound, and also quite a 'live' sound to it.

**Lee**
Stomp was a number one which was superb. It's all about getting ready on a Saturday and going out with your mates and having a wild time dancing all night. Both the song and the video had a party vibe to it and we had a ball making the video.

**Lisa**
Number one springs to mind with this song! We were so happy. Stomp has got a really fun, party feel and that's what Steps are all about. There's no deep message to our music, it's just about enjoying yourself and getting down on the dancefloor for a boogie. People relate us to party songs and I think that's why it did so well.

**Lisa**
I got my scenes done early during the first day so I got the second day off, which was lovely. A lot of what you see in the video was made up. It was spur of the moment, off the cuff, and we had a good giggle doing it. H was giving me a piggy back at one point and we were in hysterics again. I think you can tell from watching the video that we had a good time.

**H**
We wanted one of those flashing dancefloors but we couldn't get one in time, so we actually put in an entire flashing wall behind us which looked wicked.

**Claire**
The apartment the video was filmed in cost about a million, and it wasn't even that big! It was pretty gorgeous but there's no way it was worth that much.

**Lee** I was in a club one night and this song came on and I hid. I always do that when any of our songs come on when I'm out. But I love watching people doing the routines and having a good time. It's great to get a reaction from people.

**Faye**
When we were doing the dancing bit at the end we were taking the mickey and doing some really bad 80s dance routines for a laugh. If you look very closely at the video you can spot me and Claire doing some really stupid dancing. I don't know how it ended up in the final cut but it's hilarious!

**H**
I remember us being in our Winnebagos and we were called on set. The flat was about a five minute walk from where we were so we were going to stroll up there, but then it started tipping it down with rain. We couldn't walk because we would have ruined our hair and make-up so we had to hail a cab to go about two minutes up the road. God knows what the poor cab driver must have thought when us lot climbed into the back of his big black cab wearing these really bright outfits. He must have thought he was dreaming!

**Lisa**
We went quite casual for the video, which was nice. We were in jeans and sparkly tops, and I think that was the point when we started to wear more clothes that we would wear out and about every day as opposed to just stage clothes.

**Claire**
I had these sequin things stuck to my stomach and they were great. I've still got them somewhere. I get given quite a lot of stuff on shoots and stuff which is fantastic. It's always a bonus to be getting presents!

# Our Third Arena Tour

**Faye**
We went to Butlins to do the rehearsals for this, the Christmas tour, and it was a lot of fun running in and out of each others chalets and messing around. It was also very dramatic because costumes weren't ready in time and sets weren't finished. Thankfully it all got done in time in the end, though!

**H**
I rented the video of Beauty and the Beast and got inspiration for the castle that was used in this tour. I drew it and it was created like magic!

**Claire**
The Christmas tour was a bit more like a pantomime. I did enjoy it but I didn't get the same kind of feeling that I did with the tour before.

**Faye**
I liked the nice panto bit at the end with all the Christmas songs. You know how sometimes you don't really get the build up to Christmas because you're so busy? Well this was the perfect opportunity to get into the Christmas mood, and by the time Christmas came I was really excited.

**H**
We had a great build-up to Christmas on this tour and we ended on a real high. All my friends and family came to see me so we all got into the Christmas spirit together.

**Lee**
Lisa sang All I Want For Christmas Is You, and we finished the show with a Christmas medley of about four songs. We weren't sure how people would react but they absolutely loved it. We finished the tour on December 23 so we were all at home for Christmas Eve and we were buzzing by the time it came.

**Faye** The end-of-tour party was amazing. It was a karaoke bash and it was hilarious. Atomic Kitten and Boom! were there and they were such a laugh. It's always like one big party with the support acts, and they were great fun.

**Lisa** We had an end-of-tour party and it was a good way to say our goodbyes. We're like a family on tour and we knew we wouldn't be seeing people for a while, so we wanted to be able to say goodbye and Happy Christmas to each other properly. We knew we wouldn't be touring again for another year which was a sad thought because we all love touring.

**Lisa**
We used to count down the days to Christmas every night. The audience all got into the Christmas spirit and the Christmas medley went down a storm. It was like a big karaoke session!

**Lee**
Two of our dancers, Mark and Sande, opened the show playing two kids that were talking about how they wanted Steps dolls for Christmas. Then we all emerged from the boxes as Steps dolls!

**H**
I loved being in the boxes and pretending to be the Steps dolls. I thought it was such a good idea and the audience seemed to love it.

**H**
I got to perform the first song I'd written on this tour, which was called Learn To Love Again. It had an Egyptian theme and there was an amazing Egyptian backdrop and mummies and girls fanning me! Some of the male dancers carried me onto the stage on this huge flying carpet, so that was really, really cool. It was weird because no one knew the song so they were kind of sitting back and enjoying it rather than singing along. But it was a great feeling doing my own track.

**Claire**
I also sang a song which I'd written called In It For Love. I loved performing it because us girls would start off wearing suits and trilbys, and then we'd walk through this pretend mirror and suddenly we'd be wearing sparkly tops and trousers and stuff. It was fantastic.

**Lee**
I did a track called Turn Around on this tour, and I came down from the ceiling on wires which was really cool. I've got to do some pretty ace things on the tours.

**Claire**
The party on the last night in Manchester was great. It was so close to Christmas and everyone was really excited. We all had to get up the next day and go home and there were a few sore heads!

**Faye**
One of our dancers celebrated her birthday in Glasgow on that tour. We all went to this club and it was really cool because it was painted black inside, so obviously it was really, really dark and it had these bright strobe lights. That was great for us because just for that night we were anonymous. We danced all night and it was really cool to be unknown so we could go a bit wild!

**H**
I'm pretty good when it comes to partying on tour these days. I party, but I don't go out every night. I'd rather give my all on stage. I go to the gym a lot when I'm touring as well because I find that gives me a lot of strength to get through the long days. I've just had a gym fitted in my house so I've been training there a lot. It's so much easier to just get up and use my gym at home than travel somewhere. It means that I'm more disciplined and I actually go!

**Lisa**
You need a lot of stamina for touring so I went to the gym every day to keep fit. And of course the dancing keeps you fit as well.

**Claire**
With touring, I try to strike a balance between going out and relaxing and getting enough sleep. If I get too tired the show starts to suffer and I'm a mess, so I always make sure I get my beauty sleep!

# It's The Way You Make Me Feel

RELEASED: 1 JANUARY 2001 / UK PEAK POSITION: 2

**Lisa** Ahhh, I loved this. I loved the costumes and the make-up and the hair and everything. I had a long black hairpiece and we all designed our own outfits. I had a bit of a twist to mine because I didn't want it to be typical eighteenth century, I wanted it to have a bit of a millennium feel. So I had a short skirt at the front and it went into a long train at the back which I think I'd quite like for a wedding dress. It was a really beautiful blue and it's one of my favourite costumes.

**Claire**
This was a lovely video. Someone had the idea of doing a 'Dangerous Liaisons' style video. We filmed it in a huge, beautiful house called Brockett Hall. I wanted it to be a little bit more traditional so I wanted full period costumes, but we decided to make them more up to date.

**Lee**
This is probably my favourite track of all time for lots of reasons. It's a class song in itself, and we all get to sing on it and you can hear our individual voices. We recorded it in Sweden and it brings back fantastic memories of being over there.

**Claire**
This song was written especially for us by Jorgen Elofsson who wrote Sometimes for Britney. He's such a brilliant songwriter and we were so happy with it.

**Faye**
This is one of my favourite songs from Buzz and one of my favourite videos. We had it specially styled and we had lovely dresses and corsets and eccentric boots and lots of other lovely things. We all designed our costumes and were inspired by fashion magazines and what we'd seen on the catwalk.

**H**
I really liked the outfits. I think the girls all looked incredible. I had spiky hair in the video which I didn't like. Everyone told me to have a bit of a change but I soon changed it back to my normal style. I don't think it suited me at all.

**Lisa**
I loved the dancing because it was old-time mixed with some of today's influences and it looked really romantic. It was all about love triangles and we had some lovely dancers who are friends of ours in the video.

**Faye**
We had the chance to dance with all the men and it was very romantic. Us girls were having a whale of a time. It was so lovely being whisked off our feet.

**Claire**
It was nice to be able to do something different for the dance routine and I thought it was great, although it was very difficult to perform on TV.

**H** This was a two-day shoot and we got to stay overnight in Brockett Hall. It was cool because I had a massive bathroom with a huge sunken bath and a four-poster bed with beautiful views over the countryside. But it wasn't until the next morning that we were told there was a ghost there.

**Lee**
We got to do a little bit of character acting, which I liked. It was a bit like being in a movie.

**Faye**
I got to stay in The Primrose Room which was yellow – very appropriate for me!

**Claire**
I remember it got to about midnight and David wanted to shoot the single sleeve. We all stood there open-mouthed not wanting to do it because we were so shattered. We'd been up since about six that morning. My feet were killing me because I'd been in high heels, which I still can't get used to. I'm a real trainer girl. In the end we got the shoot done and it actually turned out really well and we had a laugh despite being exhausted.

## Lee

We all loved the costumes because they were something really different. But I had a necktie on and I couldn't move my neck because it was so tight. I remember the photographer Dave trying to take a picture of me and we had to do it about six times because we were both laughing – I looked so ridiculous!

# Here And Now

RELEASED: 4 JUNE 2000 / UK PEAK POSITION: 4

**Faye**
I love this song, it's another one that
we recorded in Sweden. It's done
by the same people who write for
'N Sync and Britney and loads of
other people.

**H**
I like this song because we all get
to do something on it. We all get to
play our part.

**Lee**
We all get to sing leads on this song.
I think it's got that anthemic Deeper
Shade Of Blue disco feel and people
will be playing it for a long time to
come. We had a good time going
over to Sweden and working with
different writers and producers.
I really liked Sweden. The first time
we went it was snowing and it was
beautiful. We went out clubbing
a few times and met some great
people. Everyone was so friendly
and we had a wicked time.

**Lisa**
Here And Now always goes down
well on tour and I think the video is
really funky. It's one of my favourite
songs and it's got a really cool dance
routine. It was probably quite hard
for the fans to do when they first saw
it but they soon picked it up!

**H**
The videos for Here And Now and
You'll Be Sorry are linked. At the
end of Here and Now we fly off in
this spaceship, and then You'll Be
Sorry is set inside the spaceship.
I don't think two videos have ever
been linked together like that so
we're really proud.

**Claire** I was really pleased by how the video for Here And Now turned out. It was directed by the same people that did Summer Of Love. They're primarily advert directors so they do a storyboard for each video and you just film what you need to rather than doing yards and yards of stuff that you don't need. I like that! I think it turned out wickedly with all the flowers growing out from behind us and stuff. That took us a day to film. We did a day for Here And Now and a day for You'll Be Sorry back to back.

**H**
It's funny because Here And Now
is set outside but we actually filmed
it inside on a blue screen. It was
much better because we didn't have
to worry about the weather and
stuff. I think the maze is like a
representation of love and we're
trying to find the heart which is at
the centre. I think the video is lovely
to look at, it's really arty.

**Faye**
There's a bit in the video where it
looks like I'm lying down on a hedge
but I'm actually standing up. It was
the worst thing because I kept
getting my hair stuck in the hedge!
So I'm trying to be all sultry and
concentrate on my singing and my
hair is being pulled all over the place!

**Lisa**
We filmed the video in a studio in
West London. It all ran very smoothly
even though it was early mornings
and late nights. We had to get up
at about four the first day and got
home at two the next morning.
I think we did very well to get two
videos filmed in two days. We were
all a bit delirious by the end of the
second day and we kept laughing
at really strange things.

**Claire**
We all went a bit mad at the end
of Here And Now. They sped it up
at the end and they wanted us to
dance to it sped up and it sounded
like a jungle track. H and Lee started
doing this jungle dancing and we
were all in hysterics. I think we were
so tired we went a bit mad!

# You'll Be Sorry

RELEASED: 4 JUNE 2000 / UK PEAK POSITION: 4

**Lee**
I think this is a great disco-club track. We had a great time filming the video and it gives H a chance to show off his vocals.

**Claire**
The first time I heard You'll Be Sorry it caught my attention. It's very anthemic.

**Lisa**
I think You'll Be Sorry is a really upbeat funky song, and H sounds great doing the lead vocals. Here And Now and You'll Be Sorry were the last two songs to be released from Buzz and we wanted to do a double A-side as a bit of a goodbye to the album. It's also good value for money for the fans.

**H**
The video for You'll Be Sorry reminds me of a film called Tron because it's all set in a spaceship and the colours are black and neon. I had a real cool outfit which again, I designed. I do that all the time now. Whenever I see something I like when I'm out I draw it so I can keep a record of it. I had some really cool leather trousers which had these brilliant flames on, which I loved.

**Lisa**
The video is quite American and pretty cool. I like the red and white look I had for this video, although the top did come undone during one take so we had to stop because I nearly exposed myself!

**Faye** The song is fantastic as well because it's really dancey and I love a bit of clubbing. The choreography is pretty tough but I really enjoy doing it. The crew were working on this set while we were filming the video for Here And Now. They were banging away and painting behind us and ended up working pretty much all night, bless them. There are some really cool backgrounds in the videos and I think they look stylish.

**H**
I wore sunglasses in the video but every time I turned around in the dance routine they kept flying off, so I gaffer-taped them to my eyes and nose. I put double sided tape behind my ears so that no one would see, and hid the nose part underneath the glasses. Very cunning!

**Faye**
I think the costumes are great in the videos for this and Here And Now. We had a new stylist who's a fashion designer and does a lot of catwalk stuff. We have a lot of her assistants coming down to shoots and travelling with us. We come up with ideas and stuff as well and it's great to be really involved with our outfits.

# Chain Reaction

**Lee** Diana Ross did a brilliant version of this and I hope people think that our version is as good. We've put our own stamp on it but it's still quite scary because it's always been such a strong song. But it's also a lot of fun which is what makes it very Steps. We worked with a guy called Graham who also worked on my track Turn Around. He works for Brian Rawlings who did Chers' Believe and a lot of other big tracks, so we were in good hands! And it's got a great dance routine and is sure to get people on the dancefloor.

**Claire**
I think this is a really good song. There are a lot of lyrics in it and each chorus is different. I think the Bee Gees got a bit carried away when they were writing it! I remember the song really well from when I was a kid.

**Faye**
This is a classic song and it's a great opportunity for us to record such a great track.

**H**
This is a really classic song. All the cover versions we've done have been a great success and I think we always make sure we do a good job.

# I Know We

**H**
This is kind of the girls' song. They do a cracking job on it and sound just amazing. I think the way they did it on tour was breathtaking. It went down brilliantly and there were always a few tears in the house.

**Faye**
This was a bit of a Steps girlie trip and we used to look forward to performing it every night on the Steps Into Summer Tour. It's great to do live vocals to it because you can really belt it out. It always made our mums cry. It was so weird when we performed it though. We were all in this little spotlight and I felt as if I was the only person on the stage which was a bit daunting.

**Claire**
I loved singing this on the tour when the girls and I are standing on stage belting it out, it's great. So many people told us we had to release it because they loved it.

**Lisa**
I used to get really emotional when we sang this on stage. It's such a powerful song. I'm so pleased we made it work as a trio because it's a well-known duet. I'm particularly proud of that song – my Mum used to say that it made the hairs on the back of her neck stand up!

**Claire**
I love this song. Love it. When I was at school I used to sing it with a friend of mine. Our school recorded a charity tape to raise money for a music block, and I've got this tape of me singing it when I was about 14. I don't know where it is but I hope no one finds it!

**Faye**
I don't think the boys get jealous of us girls singing on this one because they've been so busy doing their stuff. H has been doing loads of lead vocals lately, and Lee is doing incredibly well with his songwriting, so I don't think they mind at all. And they do appear on the single version, so we all do our bit.

**Lee**
We first performed this for the Abba TV tribute. We've revamped it for the single and while the girls do the lead vocals, H and I do the ad libs.

**Lisa**
This is such a great song and I don't think a lot of people know that Björn and Benny from Abba actually wrote it for Chess.

**Faye**
This is one of the first songs I remember watching on Top Of The Pops when I was younger. Barbara Dickson, who sang it with Elaine Paige, was wearing this big leopard print coat and a matching hat. It comes from the musical Chess so it's usually a bit of a show tune, but we put the Steps stamp on it.

# The Future

**Lee** There have always been rumours about us splitting up. All bands get it. And of course at some point every band is going to split up, but for us it's not going to be soon. Things are still at a peak for us and Steps are still holding their own, so why would we want to split up? We're still going strong! In fact, we've already got loads of songs written for a fourth studio album which we'll start work on after Gold, the Greatest Hits album and tour. I'd like a lot of our next album to be written by us, and we'd also like to do some producing.

### Claire

As far as the future is concerned, I just want to carry on doing what we're doing and enjoying it and be happy. I think the minute we stop enjoying it is when we have to stop, but we're still having a great time.

### Faye

We're all running around songwriting at the moment, and Lee and I have recently been to Sweden writing for the fourth album. We're getting loads of material stocked up.

### Faye

I think this year has been more settled than ever because we know exactly where we're headed. We know each other inside out now which is why we still get on so well, and I think that's one of the secrets of our success.

### Claire

We still get on as well as we always did, if not better. We're one big happy family. God, that sounds cheesy! But it really is true.

### Lisa

I think in some ways we're enjoying Steps more than ever because we've come to terms with the pressure of fame. We're getting to travel the world – we're working, partying and we're still smiling!

### H

I think we've all got things we'd love to do in the future but Steps are not splitting! Everyone thinks that because we're doing a Greatest Hits album we're saying goodbye, but we're not. It's just that all of our songs have done so well we want to do a kind of thankyou to our fans. It's like the end of the first chapter and then we're on to the next.

### Lisa

We're so excited about the Greatest Hits album because if you're a Steps fan it's the ultimate album. It's got all the hits on it and some brilliant new tracks as well.

### Lee

There's still so much we want to do in the future. We've got loads of TV presenting coming up, and there's talk of another TV show. We're also going to be spending time in America. We went out there recently and did a big television show for Nickelodeon which was great. Everyone seemed to really enjoy what we did and we had a fantastic time. We're hoping to go back for a few months next year, but we've also got so much we want to do in Britain.

### Lisa

I can't wait to go back on tour again because it's one of my favourite things about being in Steps. The tours are our project, like our little baby – we have so much input in the design of the sets, clothes and more! I'd tour all year if I could.

### Faye

I think we're all looking forward to getting back on the road again for the Greatest Hits tour. We've had a bit of a break and I think we're all missing that touring feeling a lot.

**Lisa** I think the future's really bright for us. We're still selling records and selling out tours, so people are obviously still enjoying Steps. So while our fans still want us, we'll be here. We're having the time of our lives and we still get on brilliantly. And long may it continue.

# Acknowledgments

**Photo Credits**
Courtesy of Idols Licensing and Publicity
Limited:
45, 48, 49, 98 © Jay Brooks; 111 © Ray
Burmiston; 42 © Devlin; 52, 53, 54 © Martin
Gardner; 35, 40, 59, 71, 72 © Tom Howard;
16 © Ulf Magnusson: 11, 12 © Taff Manton;
32, 33, 34, 37 © Philip Ollerenshaw; 46 © Tim
Roney; 6, 21, 23, 24, 25 © David Tonge; 4, 10,
13, 17, 31, 36, 37, 51, 53, 55, 61, 62, 63, 64, 66,
73, 76, 87, 89, 91, 92, 93, 94, 97, 99,100, 101,
107, 108, 109, 110, 113, 114, 115, 117,118,
119, 121, 125, 126, 127 © David Venni; 2, 26,
27, 29, 30, 75, 77, 78, 79, 88 © Dave Willis
© Steps:
9, 15, 18, 19, 43
© Guido Karp:
39, 57, 58, 59, 81, 82, 83, 84, 95, 128
© Jive/Zomba Records Limited:
68, 69, 103, 104, 123

The Publishers would like to thank Peter
Chadwick, Darren Hendry, Doug Hurcombe,
Simon Kenton, Carl Meek, Andrew Murabito,
Jordan Paramor, Emma Radford, Laura
Turner Laing, Zoe Wheeler and Steve Wilkins.